Along The Way
Blue Ridge Scenic

Trip Guide
Second Edition

Rick Straub

Copyright ©2008 Rick Straub
Color Version
ISBN-13 : 978-0-9793269-2-9
ISBN-10 : 0-9793269-2-3
Classic version
ISBN-13 : 978-0-9793269-5-0
ISBN-10 : 0-9793269-5-8

Published by Rick Straub
Printed in the United States
conductor_rick@windstream.net
All photo's are by Rick Straub

D0905554

Contents

Trip Date _____

All Aboard !

punch

_____

_____

_____

Autograph's

Over the last 25 years many people have been involved in bringing back the rail to the North Georgia Mountains, literally hundreds! Most were volunteers; politicians, local citizens, retirees and rail fans. People near and far played a very important part. Thank you all for your time; it was worth the effort.

I would also like to thank all those folks who helped in the preparation of this book by reviewing, correcting, providing material, feedback and support. I appreciate your help.

This book is dedicated to all the rail fans, volunteers, and staff of the Blue Ridge Scenic Railway.

I hope Y'all enjoy what I have put together in this the second edition of the trip guide.

- Conductor Rick

Introduction

Welcome to *Along the Way Blue Ridge Scenic..* We are glad you have chosen to ride with us today. Every day is a great day for a train ride!

Trip guides are not unique at all; they started when the railroads began to stretch out into remote areas and they needed to provide visitor services and increase their revenue. Works such as *Harpers New-York and Erie Rail Road Guide*, of 1855 or *Crofutt's Trans-continental Tourist Guide*, of 1872 provided a view from the rails over the countryside, man-made bridges, and viaducts that had never been imagined before. Full of advertisements that helped cover the cost of production, they were usually sponsored by the railroad. Many years later guides open a window into what life was like back then. Long distance or day trips, these places were illustrated by wonderful art work, replaced today by digital camera's that someday will serve as a snapshot of our time.

This trip guide is structured like a self-guided tour. It gives information about railroads, the Blue Ridge Scenic Railway (BRSR) line between Blue Ridge, Ga. and McCaysville, Ga. / Copperhill, Tn. and assists you with identifying points of interest. It picks up where the L&N old line leaves off with a revitalized tourist line over historic track in the North Georgia Mountains and gives some tools to make your trip informative and fun.

Train excursions have become very popular across the country in recent years. Many are staffed by volunteers who love being part of recovering the past while helping you enjoy the present. Since BRSR ran the first trip the train crew has been made up of volunteers. This guide contains information gathered from many sources over the years and has been used by the volunteers for the enjoyment of visitors, passengers, and rail fans. The 2007 operating season marked the tenth year of service. This guide is one way to celebrate the accomplishments of so many. I have made every effort to supply correct and valuable information to the reader. If you find anything incorrect and can verify facts, we would be happy to consider revising this guide.

Wilds Pierce took a railroad operating at a fraction of its former glory days and pumped life back into it. His efforts are allowing you to experience a portion of the L&N Old Line know as the "Hook & Eye". This is a great modern day achievement. In this, the second edition I have added sixteen pages, more pictures, and extended the view beyond the state line.

Many of you will be experiencing a train for the first time, others will conjure up memories while making new ones. Whichever it is sit back, relax for a moment, enjoy yourself, and the ones you're with.

Our journey today will take us from Blue Ridge, Ga. (1680 ft. above sea level) and follow the Toccoa River north descending 220 feet into McCaysville, Ga. / Copperhill, Tn. (1460 ft. above sea level). This thirteen and a half mile trip takes about one hour by rail. Depending on the time of year and amount of foliage you will get a different view on every trip. Riding in an open-air or coach car will also provide a different ride.

Let's get started!

History

The city of Blue Ridge was in its prime during the late 1800's and early 1900's. Like many other communities across this country it depended on the railroad to bring business, tourists, and travelers. Passenger service ended with the last run on February 28, 1949. The four-lane highway passed by the outskirts and many people never venture downtown. The train station was no longer the center of attention, as it once had been. More than thirty years passed before this sleepy mountain town would start its transformation back into a thriving community.

Starting around 1980 a group of citizens in Blue Ridge started work to restore the Blue Ridge Station in an effort to bring folks downtown and preserve the historic landmark. Around this time CSX Transportation Inc. (CSX) sold the 8 miles of rail between Ellijay and Blue Ridge to the State of Georgia. In 1987 CSX sold the 41 miles of track between Marietta and Tate and leased 31 miles between Tate and Ellijay to a group of investors to form Georgia Northeastern Railroad (GNRR). In 1990 the original investors sold all interests in GNRR to the current owners.

In 1988, the Great Smoky Mountain Railroad (GSMR), in Bryson City and Dillsboro, North Carolina began a successful passenger operation which suggested that running a tourist train could help save a portion of the old Atlanta to Knoxville Railroad. This section of track running between Blue Ridge and McCaysville follows the Toccoa River through some historic and scenic countryside. CSX wanted to abandon the line from Blue Ridge to McCaysville because of taxes and maintenance requirements. The Blue Ridge depot and park were acquired by the city. A group of citizens from Fannin County approached Wilds L. Pierce, the majority stockholder of Georgia Northeastern Railroad Company, Inc. (GNRR) about support to help save this portion of track and start a scenic railroad.

The management of GNRR contacted the Atlanta Chapter of the National Railroad Historical Society (NRHS) to solicit help in providing experienced excursion personnel to staff the trains. Larry Dyer and Ray Leader were able to determine that the venture had a high possibility of success and have the chapter involved again in passenger excursions. The response was to form a committee and develop a tourist railroad. Invited were two members of the Atlanta Chapter NRHS, two members from the community, and two from GNRR.

The committee worked through the details necessary to create a viable organization. An early decision was made to incorporate this entity as the Blue Ridge Scenic Railway (BRSR), a subsidiary of the GNRR. Dick Hillman, Safety Director for the GNRR was named as the first General Manager of BRSR and arranged to have the logo created which is still in use. Keith Douglas was the GNRR VP for Operations in charge of all operational areas.

In 1996 the right-of-way was acquired by the State of Georgia. On May 3, 1997, a group of railroad enthusiasts, members of the Atlanta Chapter NRHS, and local members of the North American Railcar Operators Association (NARCOA) joined GNRR to start clearing the line beyond Ellijay. Six miles of fallen limbs, kudzu overgrowth, and trees growing between the ties were cleared by hand as the first step. Then GNRR began track repair.

June 1998 was set for the first trip and just two weeks prior to opening day a many decades old wooden trestle just north of Ellijay, was "struck by lightning" and burned down leaving only two rails hanging in space. This meant all of the equipment in Tate, Ga. and Elizabeth, Ga. had to be shipped on CSX line via Cartersville, Ga. to Etowah, Tn. and then over to McCaysville, Ga. In addition vandals released handbrakes on a train at Keithsburg, Ga. that caused a derailment and destruction of two locomotives and seven grain cars. Meanwhile other efforts were continuing in preparation for the startup date.

GNRR was busy working on track repairs, purchasing and leasing passenger cars and constructing boarding areas at Blue Ridge Station and in McCaysville behind the Masonic Lodge. The Atlanta Chapter NRHS was busy recruiting, drafting the first safety manual and training volunteers to staff the trains as car hosts, conductors and trainmen. Carl Hymen was hired by GNRR as the first engineer for the BRSR. Del and Diane Kittendorf were recruited to assist with training while Diane also served as the first volunteer coordinator. Ray Leader was qualified as the first conductor and served as Chief Conductor for many years. The Atlanta Chapter's Commissary (Concession) car 206 was leased and added to the train consist. Car 206 was staffed by chapter members, with all profits going back to the Southeastern Railway Museum in Duluth, Ga.

On Saturday, May 30, 1998 the first tourist excursion was made between Blue Ridge and McCaysville as a VIP trip with a second trip on Sunday, May 31st. June 6, 1998 was opening day for operations. Initially most of the car hosts and concession crew were Atlanta Chapter members. That has shifted over the years to be mostly local volunteers. The first season consisted of 79 trips carrying 17,000 passengers.

Over the next several years the schedule has been modified with some specials runs, school trips and regular Santa Trains that always sell out. In 1998 the train consisted of three coach cars, one open-air, and one concession. In 2007 the train consisted of six coach cars, three open-air cars, and one concession.

Since that time thousands of visitors have made the trip and many found the area a great place to call home. Railroad excursions have exploded with popularity across the country as more folks look for events the entire family can enjoy; both young and old. By 2004 general building projects were underway in McCaysville, Copperhill and Blue Ridge. Now restaurants, antique shops and other businesses are once again thriving. The surrounding mountains have remained a popular vacation retreat. Cabins and property development has brought more people during the holidays and prompted special runs and extended the season for the railroad.

In the beginning the railroad brought life to this area and like so many places around the country it once again breathes life into the community. The efforts of so many over the years have paid off by preserving this piece of rail. Had this track been pulled up like the Murphy branch, it would have been lost forever but instead it continues to serve. 2007 marked the 10th season carrying 59,000 passengers.

Photo's opposite page.
Ticket Office: Glenda Page, Ann Jones, Gloria Elsner, Beverly Schaffer, Gordon Tuenge, Karen Conner, Julia Nuttinng, Mary Hyatt
Gift Shops: Ginger Yaxley, Laura Huster, Joan Shaw, Edna Duffy
Holly Strickland, Judena Beardmore, Pat Moore, Gail Hymen

ALL ABOARD!
Blue Ridge
Scenic Railway

Ticketing
Phone: 1-800-934-1898
Local: 706-632-9833
E-mail: brscenic@tds.net
www.brscenic.com

241 Depot Street
Blue Ridge, Ga. 30513

Gift Shops
Now two locations, conveniently located in the Blue Ridge Station cargo room accessible from the deck. And next door to the pavilion @ 65 Toccoa St. in McCaysville.

There are many items stocked on the concession car but for a better selection of items come by the gift shops.

Signs

There are many signs along the way. The horn, whistle, and flashing lights are a warning system that are vital to maintaining safety. The engineer's controls are on the right side of a forward moving locomotive. The Trainmen sits on the left watching for anything out of the normal. The public must co-exist with trains and it is important that everyone does their part to ensure safety. Watch for these signs along the route.

Crossings

Marked by the "W" <u>Whistle Post</u>, "X" indicates more than one. The Horn is blown four (4) times starting 1000 feet from the crossing until covered while ringing the engine bell. Recent changes by the FRA (to create a Quiet Zone) have reduced the distance between sign and crossing in an effort to reduce noise.

W

X

Speed

<u>Reduce Speed</u> signs are yellow and numbered. Speed restrictions are set by the maintenance crew.

10

<u>End Restriction</u> signs are green. Resume speed after the rear of the train has passed the green marker.

Safety, Safety, Safety –

At the beginning of each day and when changing control from one locomotive to another, the <u>Brake Test</u> sign is a caution. This indicates the train could move and everyone should stand back. At no time should anyone except the Trainmen board the train when this sign is displayed.

Mileposts

Mileposts are markers placed at one-mile intervals beginning at company headquarters and extending to the end of the line, hence the name. Since our line was part of the Louisville & Nashville Railroad (L&N), our mileposts begin at Louisville, Kn. As we depart Blue Ridge (~395.5) on our journey to McCaysville/Copperhill, the mile markers are on the west (or left) side of the train. They are white posts with a number on them.

The first milepost or marker we come to will be 395 and is located a short distance across from Mountain Street at what used to be a wood yard. From 1999 until 2005 there were about 5 log cars a week pulled south to connect with CSX. One log car can hold 5 truck loads of logs.

Markers 393/384 are really old wooden markers. They are the only two left over from the "OLD" days. Marker 385 has almost been destroyed and is now marked with a metal sign. The concrete marker is there but in bad shape.

Use the milepost to determine points along the way. Each point of interest on the next few pages will give you a number and approximate time from departure at Blue Ridge to help you find them.
Use these symbols to help determine where you are by time and mile marker.

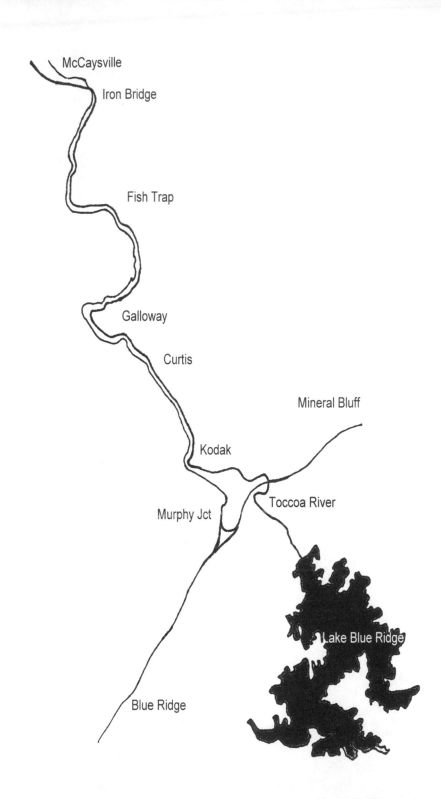

Along The Way

The Ten (10) minute warning is indicated by four (4) blasts of the train horn . O O O O

This is also the call to return from the McCaysville/ Copperhill layover.

Blue Ridge Station

The floor plan of Blue Ridge Station describes the structure almost identical to the "Standard Plan Special Combination Station" that L&N built in the early 1900's. A frame structure built in 1906 with a slate roof, weather board exterior, office and waiting rooms ceiled.

The Blue Ridge Station served cross purpose with the city as a restaurant and community center for many years. Starting around 1980, fund-raising began to refurbish this depot. The Green Thumb Project donated time, money, and labor along with senior citizens and citizens of Blue Ridge. Sandpaper and steel wool were used on the walls of the freight room and broken windows were replaced with glass from the Store House Building (now Hallmark). The Chamber of Commerce visited the depot museum in Etowah where they were given the original exterior color scheme. This is also where the 1905 build date came from that appears on the plaque out front.

Cleaning and repairs allowed the Blue Ridge Station to be the first structure in the city of Blue Ridge to be placed on historical registry (1982 - Building - #82002413). A Quilt hangs in the gift shop with all the names of the people and businesses who participated in the project to restore the Blue Ridge Train Station.

The committee was afraid that CSX Transportation would pull up the track (and dash any possibility of re-use) and they wanted the location to always look like a real train station complete with track and cars. It took the largest crane anyone had ever seen to lift the caboose from the main line to the section of rail it now sits on. Georgia DOT finally bought the track between Blue Ridge and McCaysville and leased it back to GNRR for the Blue Ridge Scenic Railway.

After the restaurant moved out in 1998 the building was once again selling train tickets. Today the entire building is used for the train tourist business but that was not always the case. It started small and grew into a facility serving thousands of guests each year coming through this small community. The freight room is now the depot gift shop. The caboose is used by the train crew and the box car is the Hometown Project office.

Flag Stop
In rural areas passengers wanting to board the train had to flag the train down in order for it to stop.

Depot
A building for the accommodation and protection of railway passengers and freight .

Station
A stopping place where trains regularly come to stand for the convenience of passengers, take on fuel, and move freight.

Train Station
A facility where passengers may board or disembark from the train and goods may be loaded or unloaded. It usually consists of one building for passengers and goods plus others associated with functioning of the railway.

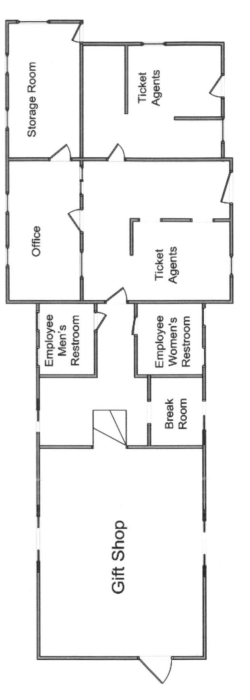

Logo

In 1998 when the BRSR logo was first created the printer said the train that appears in the center would not be very defined so it was removed. The logo was not the same without the train on it and so it was added back in 2000. The logo without the train appeared again in the 2003 brochure.

As we prepared for the 2007 season the logo was enhanced with "10th Anniversary" on the bottom and the years "1998-2007" at the top. This leaves three versions of the railway logo.

Before the 2007 season started, Ron Huster had already made changes to his jacket.

🕙 ⏱ *Murphy Junction*

Just across from the Industrial Park crossing there is a set of tracks that veer off to the right. This is Murphy Junction. The tracks run along the Hogback Ridge and go to Mineral Bluff, Ga. and at one time continued on to Murphy, Nc. The Murphy Branch supplied the only means of delivering food, clothing and rebuilding materials to Asheville, Nc. and surrounding communities after the 1916 hurricane. The tracks have been removed between Mineral Bluff and Murphy.

A "WYE" is a track arrangement with three switches and three legs for reversing the direction of a train. The intersection of Murphy Junction is where three sets of tracks come 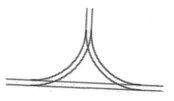 together. This unique configuration allows moving a piece of On Track Equipment (OTE) through and back out facing in a different direction. Flipping the OTE is important if a cargo door must align with a loading platform or a locomotive needs to be facing another direction.

A spur or sidetrack is a short stretch of railway used to store cars or enable trains on the same line to pass. There are several side tracks between Blue Ridge and Murphy Junction that are used for storage and building the train consist. There is only one WYE on this line.

Along The Way   21

Mineral Bluff

When the railroad arrived in 1886 the area known as Blue Ridge was just a grassy field, beautiful and natural. Mineral Bluff got the areas first train station a year after the track reached that point. A brick structure built in 1887 was influenced by locals to support a large tannery and timber products. Visitors would come for the healthy mineral springs and inspirational spa retreats. The track ends just beyond the depot, removed between here and Murphy, Nc. What was once a main line is now a branch line used occasionally for storing rolling stock. The depot has been refurbished but you will have to drive to Mineral Bluff a short distance up the highway to see the renovations.

Hogback Ridge Road followed the rail to Mineral Bluff but now the bridge is no longer passable. One side sits on private property out of reach of visitors.

Kodak Moment

Twenty minutes out we come to what is referred to as the "Kodak Moment". This point in our travel is located at mile marker 392, which is only a short distance beyond what used to be a "Petting Farm." This is the point in which we first encounter the Toccoa River. It is called the "Kodak Moment" because it is quite picturesque and you can see both up and down the river as it is in a sharp curve to the right.

Appalachia (ap-uh-LAl-chee-uh)

The Appalachia Mountain region is an area of 200,000 square miles that follows the spine of the Appalachia Mountain range from Maine to Alabama in the eastern part of the United States. A blanket of foliage acts like a sponge collecting moisture from high elevations. The peaks, slopes, and rolling hills slowly release water into creeks and streams to form rivers in the valley's below. The waters of the North Georgia Mountains in the northeast portion of the state form the Hiwassee River system. The Hiwassee River flows north into North Carolina then turns west into Tennessee where it meets up with the Tennessee River. The Hiwassee river system includes Hiwassee, Ocoee, Nottley, Valley, and Toccoa rivers.

River flows north

Many visitors notice the river flows north. I have also been told there are only a few rivers in the world that flow north, the Toccoa is one of them. Why does the river flow north? We started our trip in Blue Ridge at about 1680 feet elevation above sea level and descended to 1460 feet. Very simply gravity.

Curtis Switch

Curtis Switch Road is a gated crossing. Once a meeting place for north and south bound trains it had a side track where one train could wait for the other to pass. Just beyond the road on the right is an old foot bridge for crossing the river.

Flashing red lights, lowered crossing gates, and a ringing bell at a road crossing are classic warnings associated with railroads. There are three gated crossings where you can wave to the waiting cars.

Head on Collision
On July 8, 1928, around 8:51 PM there was a head-end collision between two L&N passenger trains about a mile south of Curtis. North bound Train #6 pulled by Engine 139 collided with south bound Train #7 pulled by Engine 137 which resulted in the death of an engineer. At the time it was a single-track line operated by timetables and train orders.

A single track between Blue Ridge and McCaysville means that coordination must be made to insure two pieces of equipment do not occupy it at the same time. An <u>Absolute Block</u> is a block (area between two mile markings) that may be occupied by only one train at a time. Absolute Block authority is granted to BRSR for movements in both directions. This means that no other equipment will share the track with us today.

Watch for mile post 390 on the way back to Blue Ridge. There will be a perfect photo opportunity just past Curtis Switch Road. The track sweeps to the right and then back to the left for a view of the entire train.

(36) *Galloway*

388.5

A short distance from Curtis Switch Road (about 1½ miles) at what would be mile marker ~388.5 the river curves to the right. This low area is reported as having the first white settlers in the area. William Galloway came to the area in 1822 and raised his family working as an Indian agent. There was a post office here from 1901 until 1920. Not only did the river supply fish for food, in addition to what could be grown, but also transportation.

In 2003 the railroad arranged for volunteers to have a picnic on this site by the river.

Plant Life

I will never claim to know much about plant life. Each trip, however, I see something new. I thought it would be a nice idea to add a few of the more common sightings. See what you can find along the track.

Azalea   Black eyed Susan   Fern

Thistle   Joe-Pye   Kudzu

Rhododendron   Goldenrod   Mtn. Laurel

𝒇𝒊𝒔𝒉 𝒥𝒓𝒂𝒑

387

Between mile post 386 and 387 we come to the "Fish Trap". This is one of the most interesting and fascinating sights on our trip. It is constructed of river rock from both sides of the river about a third of the way across the river, and then a deep "V" is formed pointing downstream. It is not known exactly who or when "Fish Traps" were constructed. They were in the rivers when the first settlers came to the area. It is generally accepted that early Indians would enter the river upstream, then walk, splash or in other ways cause a commotion in the water, causing the fish to swim downstream to get away from the commotion. The fish would be concentrated in the "V" area where they could be caught in nets and baskets. Fish Traps are not unique to our river. They were common in most of the rivers across the southeast.

Occasionally when the water is high, usually controlled by Blue Ridge Dam, it's a little harder to see.

(46) 🕐

Kyle

385.2

According to a 1920 L&N time table. Approximately 51.2 miles south of Etowah, Tn. lies the flag stop of Kyle. This is about 1.2 miles before the iron bridge at mile 385.2. The settlement was named after Henry S. Kyle who was the first postmaster when the U.S Postal Department approved the location in 1890. The post office closed in 1909 and services were transferred to Galloway.

Fellow volunteer Bill Purdy tells me there was a siding that could hold 15 cars (630 feet) on the east side of the track north of Kyle Creek, which flows into the Toccoa River. Track maintenance has covered some of the old siding. Development grading and gravel have almost eliminated any remnants of a village.

A stacked rock mound still remains on the west side of the track in the woods; only viewable when the leaves have fallen. This may have been the foundation of a grist-mill or dam.

Toccoa Bridge

At mile marker 384 we cross the Toccoa River on our way to McCaysville/Copperhill. Markers 384 along with 393 are wooden markers as discussed earlier. The railroad, then known as the M&NG (Marietta and North Georgia), reached McCay in the summer of 1889. The route of the railroad was to be from Marietta, Georgia to Knoxville, Tennessee. With crews working both north, from Marietta, and south, from Knoxville, the two sections of track were joined on June 30, 1890 amid much celebration.

On July 4, 1890 a passenger train traveled the entire line from Marietta to Knoxville for the first time. Regularly scheduled service began on August 18, 1890. The M&NG became the AK&N (Atlanta, Knoxville and Northern) Railroad in the late 1890's and then in 1902 the line was purchased by the L&N (Louisville and Nashville). In 1905 the L&N began a program of upgrading the newly acquired railroad which included replacing the bridge across the Toccoa River south of Copperhill. This bridge is of heavier construction than other bridges along the line.

The bridge spanning the Toccoa River offers a beautiful view both up and down the river as you cross. During the summer months you can wave to rafters and tubers enjoying the water ride.

McCaysville/Copperhill

Just as the river changes its name at the state line, so does the name of this small mountain community. McCaysville/Copperhill grew up around the railroad and mines a few miles away. The mines produced copper, iron, sulfur, zinc and small amounts of gold and silver. Before 1900 the Copper Basin was the largest mining district in the Southeast. The mines have long since gone (closed in 1989) but the town is still serving visitors and tourists. In 1990 the area suffered a great flood when the banks of the river overflowed flooding several feet up building walls.

A favorite for travelers is to take a picture while standing in two states at the same time using the painted line in the IGA parking lot. Today there are shops and restaurants to visit while in town. Be sure to get a walking map to assist your tour.

Upon anticipation of the train a loading area was constructed behind the Masonic Lodge. Steps on the north side provided access to the sidewalk. The Blue Ridge Scenic Railway McCaysville pavilion (75 Toccoa Ave.) was opened in the summer of 2005. The old house that occupied this space was replaced by a facility much more suited to the visitor providing rest rooms and tables. It has a wooden ramp to the sidewalk.

McCaysville/Copperhill is as far as the regular BRSR trip goes. The 2007 schedule Included a few special trips venturing farther north over Hiwassee loop with the cooperation of the TVRR.

Along The Way

Hook and Eye

The famous Hook and Eye Division of the Louisville & Nashville Railroad (L&N) was the first to tackle the Appalachian Barrier in the south. It gets its name from two engineering feats. At a time in the south after the Civil War when money was in short supply, curves were cheaper than cuts.

The "Hook" is a 15-degree double reverse-curve at Tate Mountain, in Georgia that took four miles of track to gain two and a half miles "as the crow flies" between Talking Rock and Whitestone.

The "Eye" is a spiral loop, 7/8 mile long, that crosses under itself and comes very close to crossing itself twice as it traverses Bald Mountain in Tennessee. A 1940 Railroad Magazine article Hook and Eye Division, by H.G. Monroe, states "Where else can a hogger watch the rear of his train with as little effort as on the Hook and Eye?" It was built around 1898 replacing six miles of reckless rail constructing the great "W switchback" that allowed the rail to drop seventy five feet to the bank of the Hiwassee River. Before the loop only 4 cars at a time could be shuttled between each leg.

Very few features of this type existed on a U.S railroad at the time but the Eye still exist today. In 2007 with the cooperation of the Tennessee Valley Railroad Museum working with their Hiwassee River Rail Adventures ("HRRA"), the Blue Ridge Scenic Railway scheduled trips to Gee Creek, Tn. over this historic and famous Eye portion of the old L&N "Hook and Eye Division" track.

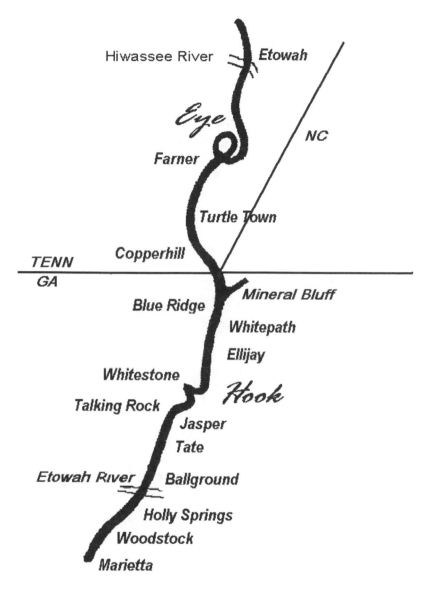

The "Hook & Eye" Division

This image was redrawn based on a drawing that appeared in the 1940 magazine article by H.G Monroe

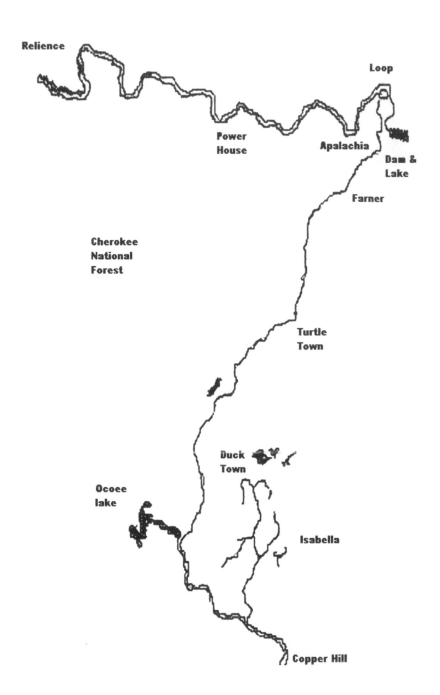

Relience

Loop

Power
House

Apalachia

Dam &
Lake

Farner

Cherokee
National
Forest

Turtle
Town

Duck
Town

Ocoee
lake

Isabella

Copper Hill

Copper Country

This section was inspired by the special activities that celebrated the 10th operating season.

Carley Straub photo

A New Adventure

On Monday, May 7, 2007 a group of 266 Passengers (volunteers and guests) and 20 crew members took the trip over the Hiwassee loop from Blue Ridge Ga. to Gee Creek Tn. We started at 10AM with two concession cars, five coach cars, two open cars, and two locomotives (both on the North end). Running our normal trip to McCaysville, we arrived at the Tn. state line where a crew from the Tennessee Valley Railroad (TVRR) took over.

We pulled into the side tracks across from the chemical plant where two locomotives (CSX 4439 and TVRR 710) were waiting for us. A box lunch occupied passengers while the equipment was reconfigured and then we were off again, pulled by four locomotives. The tracks are less curvy and the speeds were much faster than we were used to. Taking pictures took more skill at 20 MPH. There were more trees than along the Toccoa River because this is the Cherokee National Forrest, the mountain scenery is beautiful.

Copperhill at mile marker 382, is 1460 feet above sea level. We climbed to 1720 feet at Stanbury (marker 373), just beyond Ducktown, before we started our decent. Gee Creek (marker 341) is 748 feet above sea level. Going north, downhill was interesting as we crossed over the track we would soon be traveling. On the famous Hiwassee loop at Bald Mountain, you can see the track below. We looped around and under the bridge although our train was not long enough to see the "bottom end" (rear of train) above us.

The forty five mile trip took about 3 hours from Copperhill. We had a pretty good view of the

Apalachia Dam, looking down through the trees. There are several spots where speeds slowed to 5 and 10 MPH as we curved around rocks and squeezed through passes. The Apalachia Power Station gave us a great view of the river. The water was shallow, and the rock lining the bottom looked like mud flats in many spots. We crossed the river at Reliance and finished up at Gee Creek Park.

It was a good time for everyone, seeing a new section of track, visiting with friends and continuing the tradition of BRSR outings. 2007 was the first year we partnered with TVRR on special combination trips. TVRR runs this route regularly throughout their operating season. Look them up if you are interested in more railroading adventures. (Tvrail.com)

Copper Basin

In the lush forest where the states of Georgia, Tennessee, and North Carolina meet, rust-colored hills revealed a valuable resource. Mining would continue for over a hundred years fueling the industrialization of the United States, and changing the landscape forever. State-of-the-art practices of the times proved to be brutal on the environment, characterized as denuded landscape, without the natural or usual covering.

In the 1880's the railroads provided a means to transport goods cheaply and was the key to large scale logging. Timber was extracted in all but remote places to be used for homes, furniture and fuel. As logging companies moved on the land was sold at rock-bottom prices. Lowlands were bought for farming while the higher elevations became national forests. During the 1930's trees were replanted and dams were built to control flood waters. Today tourism is the most rapidly growing industry.

Just eight miles north of Copperhill, Tn. is the location of all mining in the area; it is known as the "Copper Basin." Ducktown and Isabella were boomtowns in 1854 when mining was in full operation. Over the years the area would see good  times and bad as production stopped and restarted again. The railroad came just at the right time.

The process known as "open heap roast smelting" used large amounts of trees for fuel to separate ore while fumes from the smoke came down as acid rain killing the vegetation. This denuded land-scape was eroded by the rains. Contaminants left by mining companies are still being discovered. There are major efforts underway to clean up the area and make it usable again for walking trails and recreation.

The mines have been closed since 1989, but there are still plenty of local residents who grew up around copper mining. The mining companies provided everything from housing to clothing and furnishings to its employees. Remnants of their way of life are preserved and are on display at the Ducktown Copper Basin Museum. Pictures and artifacts tell a story of life in a mountain mining town you cannot get anywhere else.

The train does not go to Ducktown, but it's just a short drive from Copperhill, Tn. on route 68.

Welcome to the Copper Basin!

cApalachia Dam and Power House

The Apalachia Dam (spelled with a single p) project was the last dam built in the series. It was started in 1941 and finished in 1943 to generate power during WWII. The dam stands 150 feet high and is about 1300 feet across the Hiwassee River to form Apalachia Lake.

The powerhouse for this system is located 12 miles downstream or 8.3 miles across the mountain pass. An aqueduct with an 18-foot diameter tunnel system supplies water for the two turbines at the powerhouse. Arial maps from satellite views show traces of the route through changes in the tree line. Water is gravity-fed from an elevation of about 1270 feet above sea level at the dam to around 1145 feet above sea level at the powerhouse, a drop of around 125 feet. The design creates 440 feet of head water.

The Apalachia dam is visible through the trees on the lower right side as we approach the loop from the south. The generating capacity is 93,600 kilowatts at the powerhouse, but you will have to wait to see the facility as we go around the loop and continue downstream.

From the Tennessee state line downstream to the Highway 411 bridge is designated Tennessee State Scenic River. This includes a seventeen mile trout management section between the Apalachia power-house and Patty Bridge.

To get a photo like this of the dam, you will need to visit by car.

Robert Bracket
power house
photo's

The Loop

At bald mountain the track crosses over itself (1400 feet above sea level) by way of a wooden trestle. You can see the track below (1220 feet above sea level) as we spiral down.

The loop was built to replace a switch back in 1898. A switch back is a section of track shaped like a "W". The switch back allows the train to traverse the elevation at smaller increments. Each section is separated by a switch and it could only handle several cars at a time creating an inconvenient solution. The loop however is a continuous section that handles the 180 feet elevation quicker and easier. Traffic grew as the mines in Copperhill shipped products by rail. In 1906 the route to Cartersville was opened and traffic south was reduced over the old line.

As we proceed west away from the dam there is not much of the river. The dam channels water to the power house by pipe. This is national forest so you can expect a lot of trees. The forest is still very young. After logging stripped the landscape clean it took reforestation efforts of 1930's to bring back the foliage. That means the trees are less than a hundred years old.

As the train descends from its high elevation moving west the river will also build again into natural fish reserves.

Below, Robert Bracket bridge photo

Continuing west we cross the Hiwassee River at Reliance (marker 354), approaching Gee Creek, Tn.

An upgrade to the power house necessitated north-end track reconditioning in 2004. An Iron reclaiming project in Copperhill necessitated reconditioning the south-end. With a fully maintained line the stage was set for some tourist excursions.

Ten years ago who could have imagined that two trains would arrive in McCaysville/Copperhill at the same time loaded with passengers? The TVRR comes from the north and BRSR from the south. Two trains unloading hundreds of tourists on this small community. The area continues its tradition of welcoming visitors and taking pride in its history.

McCaysville was like many areas in the United States that fell on hard times in 1920's. Work picked up during WWI and WWII. The TVA project used the track to build the Apalachia Dam and Power House in 1941. It was revitalized by L&N in the 1960's and again by two upgrade projects around 2004. The track was built in the 1880's and is now over one hundred and twenty years old and still serving.

The route from Gee Creek to Copperhill is a regular feature of TVRR. Pick up a brochure around town or visit the museum in Etowah.

The "Tennessee Valley Authority" Act of 1933 created a corporation to manage the resources of the

Tennessee River system. The TVA project built a series of dams on the Hiwassee river system during WWII for national defense, agriculture, industrial development, and to control destructive flood waters. These dams formed Hiwassee Lake, Apalachia Lake, Nottely Lake, Blue Ridge Lake, and Chatuge Lake. Much of this area is protected by a national park system that includes Chattahoochee National Forest in Georgia, Nantahala National Forest in North Carolina, and Cherokee National Forest in Tennessee.

Once part of the Cherokee Nation, today the river system serves thousands of visitors who come to fish, swim, and enjoy the beautiful out doors. Several railroads stil offer tourist excursion trips along old routes through mountain passes otherwise not accessible.

Typical Consist from south to north

On-Track-Equipment	8704 or 2000	*106	*105	2705	*549	114 or 206	*332	150	2975	*2929	697	7529 or 7562
Seating	2	50	50	60	56	~	50	65	70	70	45	3
Type	L	C	C	C	C	B	C	C	O	O	O	L

L = Locomotive, **C** = Coach, **B** = Baggage Concession, **O** = Open-Air

* Restrooms

The Consist

(pronounced CON-sist) the cars which make up a train.

Each vintage car is different, which makes it unique with its own history. While on board the train feel free to visit the Concession (Commissary) car where you will find drinks, snacks, and souvenirs.

Snow Train

It was a winter morning in the mountains like many others. My wife Rae Ann and daughter Carley were hoping for snow. About 8 a.m. Sunday morning we awoke to flurries that quickly subsided; just another teaser. The plan was for them to go back to Atlanta while I worked the train and followed later. They left about 9 a.m. and the snow started to fall again about 9:30 a.m., it didn't stop for what seemed like hours.

Several inches fell quickly and continued once a base had formed. Making my way to Blue Ridge would be slow and cautious. Erma Gladieux was the office manager and took this wonderful picture of the south end of the train that appeared in the 2001 brochure and calendar. Many reservations were cancelled but the scheduled trip departed Blue Ridge station on time. All of the businesses were closed including the ticket office so everyone could go for a snow ride.

Notice the tracks are showing through the snow and what has collected on the nose of the locomotive appears to be slipping. By departure time the temperature was high enough to start the snow melting even though flurries continued. By the time the train got back to Blue Ridge Station that afternoon 80% of the snow had melted into streams of water running down the roads. Since that day my family and I have not seen a repeat of the amount of snow on a single day in the mountains, however, we are still hopeful.

Photo by Erma Gladieux

ℒocomotives

A new breed of workhorse, the "chopped-nose" GEEP was introduced in the 1950's by General Motors - Electro Motive Division (GM-EMD).

In the Georgia Northeastern Railroad (GNRR) fleet, we at the BRSR have used locomotives GNR-7529 at the north end of the consist pulling us to McCaysville and GNR-7562 at the south end pulling us back to Blue Ridge. Some day it would be nice to do some switching at each location but for now there is no place to run around so we will pull out, change locomotive control and pull back. That's why there is a locomotive at each end. Both units came from Conrail.

Between 1954 and 1959 GM-EMD produced a number of model GP9 , 1750 HP locomotives. In 1976 Conrail inherited a fleet of GP9 locomotives from Penn Central that were rebuilt as GP10's. GNR-7529 started out as New York Central NYC-5958, later renumbered to PC-7358 by Penn Central, CR-7358 by Conrail, and then CR-7529 as a GP10. GNR-7562 started out as Pennsylvania Railroad PRR-7098, later renumbered to CR-7098 by Conrail, and then CR-7562 as a GP10.

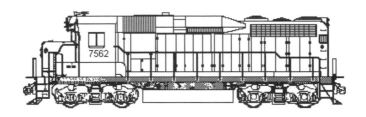

Front Cover photo by Rick Straub. 2002 GNRR locomotive 7562 sitting idle at rock quarry in White Path

The Consist

Coach 105/106

Coach 106 was one of 42 10-roomette, 6 bedroom sleepers "ten-six sleepers" built by Pullman Standard and delivered to the Florida East Coast (FEC) Railroad in September of 1949. It carried the name "Oriente" until purchased by the Canadian National (CN) Railroad in 1967 when FEC cut passenger service. Renamed "Grande Riviere" and eventually converted to present long-distance coach configuration. The number CN/VIA 5740 is still evident on the inside doors at the end of the car. Later CN sold it to Bangor & Aroostook Railroad where it was renamed BAR 106.

In 2001 coach 106 was acquired by Blue Ridge Scenic Railway to be used as first-class service. Originally it was powered by 114 volts D.C. provided by batteries and a genemotor driven by a 480v, three-phase A.C. motor. The genemotor was driven by the rotation of the cars axles through gears while the car was underway.

BRSR converted to an onboard diesel powered generator in 2001 using employees of GNRR, contractors, and volunteers. It was extensively rewired and air-conditioning system completely replaced. Coach 105 is a sister to 106. These 80ft. cars seat 50 passengers .

Photo's by Larry Heron

The Consist

Coach 2705

Coach 2705 is one of three cars purchased from the Long Island Railroad (LIRR) when it was retired in 1999. It has its own generator for heat and air-conditioning.

It was built by Pullman-Standard in 1963 as a 130 seat MU (cab control) commuter coach. In 1973, it was converted to an 86 seat coach commuter bar (push-pull).

Some cleaning was performed and modifications made to fit our needs. Originally it had a 3/2 seating configuration with five seats across. Many of the seats were removed to allow more leg room than was needed for a commuter as well as increasing the center aisle width by using only two seats on each side. The excess seats that came from modifications to cars 2705/2929/2975 were used in Coach 332 to make it more comfortable. The brown exterior was changed to blue in 2007 to march the consist colors.

Look for the New York State seal pattern imprinted in the ceiling.

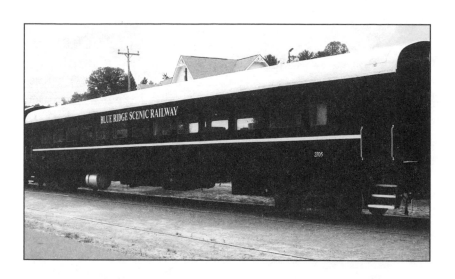

Photo by Larry Heron

Coach 549

Coach 549 was purchased by Blue Ridge Scenic Railway in 1998 from Greensboro, Nc. Chapter of the National Railway Historical Society (NRHS). This passenger car was built 1938 by Budd Mfg. for the Atchison, Topeka and Santa Fe Railroad. It operated in various passenger train assignments including the famous Santa Fe Super Chief, operating between Chicago and Los Angeles, until being sold to Penn Central Railroad. Its last regular service was with New Jersey Transit in commuter service into New York City until being retired and sold to the Greensboro, North Carolina chapter of the NRHS.

Since the car has been in the BRSR consist several modifications have been made. Two additional restrooms are located at the north end and a storage room at the south end now houses the air system. Ceiling fans were added before the air-conditioning was replaced.

Photo's by Larry Herron

Special Access 405

Special Access 405 is being modified to allow passengers in wheel chairs and special boarding needs to experience the trip.

The car was one of an order of 16 cars built by Pullman-Standard in July 1947, for the Bangor & Maine Rail Road (B&M). Its original configuration was a 56-seat coach, 10-seat smoker. A glass partition separated the rooms. On the B&M it carried the name Snowbird and was numbered 4807. In 1957, it was acquired by the Wabash Rail Road and renumbered 1424. In 1968 it became part of the Norfork & Western Rail Road where it was again renumbered 1831. In 1969 it was converted to a air brake instruction car and renumbered 405.

During this conversion it had most of the windows on the coach end covered and air brake stands installed for use in training. In 1990, the car was acquired by the GNRR and used until 2007 as an office and dispatch facility at its Elizabeth Yard.

Early in 2008 Carl Hyman headed the project to reconfigure 405 so that it could be added to the BRSR consist by spring. The design would include a lift on either side and partially open air. Photo's were taken in January 2008 during the first stage.

History by Larry Dyer

Snow Bird

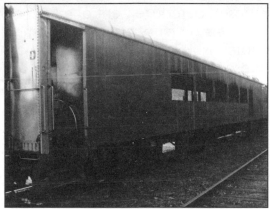

Concession 206

Concession car 206 was built for the Northern Pacific Railroad as part of an order of 10 baggage cars numbered 200 thru 209. It was ordered in November 1955 and delivered in May 1956 by Pullman-Standard. It is 70 ft. long with two double axle trucks. In 1958 it had a small bathroom (messenger) installed in the center of the car. Northern Pacific retired the car from active service in 1971 but held onto it and used it occasionally as a commissary (concession) car in excursion service for approximately 10 years and then sold it to a passenger car dealer in Portland, OR.

In the mid-1980s, following a derailment of the Norfolk Southern (NS) steam excursion fleet, the company imposed a requirement of roller bearings and tight-lock couplers on all excursion equipment. The Atlanta Chapter, NRHS had a commissary car that did not meet these new requirements and was forced to purchase a new commissary car, which was 206. When purchased, the car was painted in Burlington Northern green and had no generator, AC or counters in it. The car was used in NS steam excursion and New Georgia RR trips until both programs ended in late 1994. The car was leased to the Blue Ridge Scenic Railway in 1998 and used for three seasons. The Atlanta Chapter has had the car on its property since then as a gift shop and now it's back. Car 206 was purchased by Blue Ridge Scenic Railway as the second concession car in 2006.

Ever since acquiring commissary car 206 in 2006 folks have been having some fun with what was stenciled on the undercarriage "**DO NOT HUMP**".

There are two different types of railroad yards, flat and hump yards. In a hump yard, a hill is made so that the engines can push the cars up and across, and when they reach the top, they're uncoupled and allowed to drift down the correct track by gravity to the train that they will go out on. A worker in a nearby tower use buttons or levers to throw switches and direct it to the proper train.

The problem with hump yards is that coupling is often quite rough and fragile items can be broken. It was typical to have "DO NOT HUMP" stenciled on office cars, dining cars and any other car with fragile items so they would not be sent down to a rough coupling. The reason they're used is that it's faster than having an engine gently connect each car.

Concession 114

The Brittany, Concession car 114 on the consist was manufactured by National Steel Car Co in May, 1958 for the Canadian National Railway Co. as car CN/VIA 9293. In 1974 it was renumbered to CN/VIA 9664. When it was eventually bought by the Bangor & Aroostook Railway Co in Maine when it became BAR 114.

The car was purchased by Blue Ridge Scenic Railway in 2000 to act as its concession car. In April 2001, it was revamped with counters and coolers to its current configuration by volunteers. The concession is essential to the train consist. It contains the communications center, souvenirs, drinks and snacks (popcorn and candy). Connected to land power by night it also carries its own generator. It has gated sliding doors on each side. Until 2006 it was connected between 332 on the north end and 549 on the south end. The hand brake was used while standing in McCaysville.

In 2006 when concession car 206 was added to the consist, the Brittany saw less activity. Currently it sets on a storage track, only used occasionally for special trips.

The Brittany

Coach 332

Coach CSXT 972332 (commonly referred to as 332) was purchased by Blue Ridge Scenic Railway after being retired from service by CSX Transportation. Built by American Car Foundry in 1955 as a 60 seat divided (probably Jim Crow) coach for the L&N RR. It was acquired by Amtrak in 1971, retired in 1976 and sold to CSX for work train service and numbered 972332. It may have been one of the last "Jim Crow" cars built. It was restored to coach service in 1998 as one of original cars in the BRSR consist.

Before renovations by BRSR it had no seats so we installed bus seats for a couple of years. Since then a few changes have been made by the volunteers. The seats were replaced by excess ones pulled from the Long Island Commuter cars and the table was split in two with each half attached to a side. Restrooms were added to the north end and shelves with baby changing area was added to original restroom space. Coach 332 is used for the crew briefing before each scheduled trip. It is connected to the north end of the concession car and its generator supplies electricity to coach 150 and the open-air cars to the north of the consist. The brown exterior was changed to blue in 2007 to match the consist colors.

Toccoa River

Larry Herron photo

The Consist   69

Coach 150

Coach 150 (Lake Blue Ridge) was originally built for New York Central Railroad, in 1923 by Osgood Bradley Company which was later taken over by Pullman. This car was purchased by Blue Ridge Scenic Railway in 1998 from Gettysburg Railroad.

The car has "walk-over" seats so the direction of the car could be changed at the end of the line but have been tied down so they don't get worn-out. The upholstery has been refinished and the windows are now locked down to avoid injury and allow the heat and air (that was recently added) to work properly. The 80 ft. car was originally built as a self-propelled electric commuter car with controls in the Vestibule. It had open windows in the summer and electric baseboard heat in the winter. It got power from a thin rail beside the regular rail. On the north end you can identify where a window has been covered with a metal plate on the left side. A jump seat folds out of the wall on the right side.

A railroad coach with pairs of seats on each side of the center aisle, and open interior are know as 'American Style' coach. Coach 150 seats 65 passengers and the closest restroom is on 332 to the south. The brown exterior was changed to blue in 2007 to match the consist colors.

Larry Herron photo

The Consist

Open-Air 2975/2929

Open-Air cars 2929 and 2975 were among three Pullman-built push-pull coaches (2929, 2975, and 2705) purchased from the Long Island Rail Road (LIRR) when they were retired in 1999. In 1954, the LIRR ordered twenty-five 120-seat commuter cars from Pullman-Standard. An additional fifty-five identical cars were ordered in June 1955. The first order, car numbers 2901-2925, were delivered from Pullman-Standard's Osgood Bradley plant in Worcester, Mass. in June, 1955 as lot 6961, drawing W-52607 .

Two LIRR cars 2929 (Ridge Runner) and 2975 (River Breeze) were converted to open-air by volunteers Scottie Wershing, Joe Beardon, Carl Hymen and Chuck Nutting. Torches were used to remove the car's 24 double windows and to cut larger openings in order to widen the view. They used torches but didn't know what to expect so they had fire extinguishers and water buckets ready. Extra support posts were welded in place as well as safety rails along the sides to fully transform it to an open-air car. Existing seats were removed and replaced with steel framed, padded benches that run lengthwise through the middle of the car. Coach 2705 remains in its original design although some of the seats were removed for more comfort. Look for the New York State seal pattern imprinted in the ceiling.

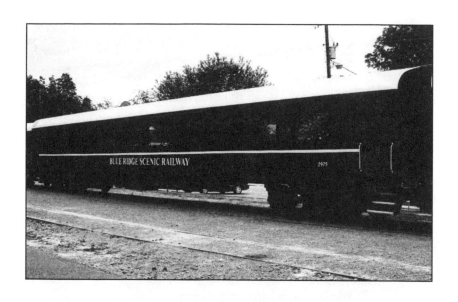

Larry Herron photo

The Consist

Open-Air 697

Our first open-air car was purchased from The Great Smoky Mountain Railroad in 1998. We lovingly refer to it as 697. The Alarka Creek is a 40 ft. box car built in 1971. Converted to open-air coach with retractable stairs on each side and seating down the middle facing outwards. As with all cars it has its own unique ride, sitting closest to the north engine it relays the sounds of the bell, horn and rails better than any other car. Car 697 was originally isolated from the rest of the train. Car hosts had to keep a cooler to sell drinks and passengers had to wait until the end of each trip to use any facilities.

The steps were lowered and raised by a hand crank until they were removed prior to the 2005 season. In 2004 a walkway was fashioned to connect the car to the rest of the consist and passengers are no longer restricted to the car. The first cars to fill up are always the open-air cars so 697 is regularly filled to capacity.

Car 697 gets the most of the coupling action as well. It couples to the north locomotive to pull the train off the house track. When trainman training is performed car 697 is used for practice coupling. The brown exterior was changed to blue in 2007 to match the consist colors.

Alarka Creek

Larry Herron photo

The Consist 75

✐ Horn Signals

SOUND	SIGNAL (HORN) INDICATION
0 = short —- = long	Blast Meaning
0	Applying air brakes
— —	Proceeding releasing air brakes
0 0	Acknowledging any signal not otherwise provided for
0 0 0	Backing up
0 — —	Acknowledging train order signal displayed for delivery of orders
0 0 0 0	Calling for signals (10 minutes warning)
— — 0 —	Approaching public crossings at grade, tunnels, yards, or other points where men may be at work and when passing the rear of freight trains
0 —	Inspect train for a leak in brake pipe system or for brakes sticking
Succession of short sounds	Warning to people and/or animals

✐ Railroad Safety

The Cross Buck sign is a warning to the public of a rail crossing. Some crossings have gates, lights and bells to warn the public of an oncoming train. Often we forget that train tracks are private property, here long before other vehicles, and trains always have the right of way. When crossing tracks at designated locations we need to be conscious of safety.

Vintage Railroad

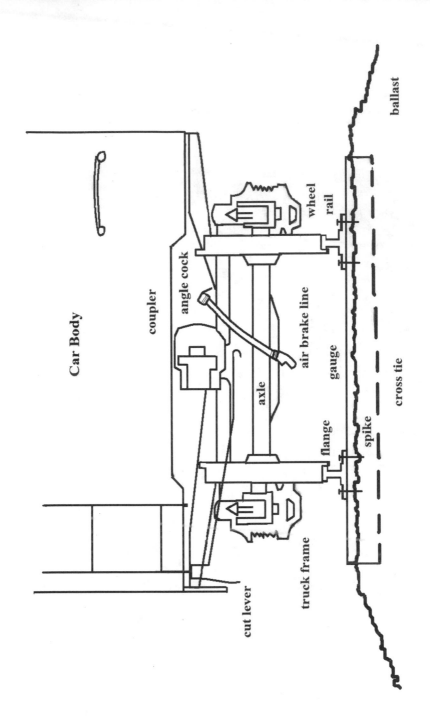

Car Body

coupler

angle cock

cut lever

truck frame

axle

air brake line

flange

gauge

spike

wheel

rail

cross tie

ballast

Component Descriptions

Angle cock - Pipe valve that controls flow of air in brake system.

Air Brake Hose - Links the cars brake system together.

Ballast - Crushed rock used to keep track aligned and properly drained.

Coupler - A moveable knuckle that locks when two cars come together.

Cross Tie - Treated wood or concrete used to attach plate that hold rail in place.

Flange - Small lip on inner edge of the wheel

Gauge - Distance between inner head of rails

Knuckle – movable portion of the drawbar coupler.

Rail - Formed high quality steel. Three parts are head, web, and base. Standard length is 39' connected by bolts but the new standard is continuous welded rail (CWR)

Spike - Steel piece driven through plates to hold rail in place

Track - Straight or curved pair of rails. Curves are usually 1 or 2 degrees. The slope or grade is measured in distance climbed per distance traveled

Wheel - Connected to an axle forming a wheel set. Cars have 8 wheels in two sets called trucks.

Trains can move at anytime; never crawl under or between cars. This is one of the most dangerous things anyone can ever do and we see more adults do it every year. It is so important to slow down and think about your actions. The result could ruin a perfectly good day for everyone. it is dangerous and stupid to go under a train.

Air Brakes

The first train brakes required a brakeman. To stop a train the engineer would blow a certain pattern with the whistle and the brakemen would move from car to car setting handbrakes. The first air brakes used a compressor and a pipe running the length of the train. In this direct brake system, when the brake pipe was pressurized the brakes went on.

The modern air brakes have an inverted behavior of the direct brake. By pressurizing the brake pipe or charging the system causes the brakes to release. A triple valve is attached to the brake pipe, then to a reservoir, and to the brake cylinder. As air is pumped by the locomotive, the triple valve directs it into the car's reservoir. When fully charged the reservoirs will be at a pressure of 70 pounds. We test the brakes before every trip ensuring the ability to apply and release on all cars.

To apply the brakes the air is removed from the brake pipe. When the reservoir air pressure is greater than the brake pipe pressure it moves the triple valve and allows pressure into the brake cylinder, and the brakes apply.

To release the brakes an increase in pressure greater than the 70 pounds in the reservoir causes the triple valve to a position that allows air in the brake cylinder to escape and the brakes are released. In essence, the brakes are always applied; it takes effort to release them. By placing the train into emergency the air in the brake pipe is instantly released causing rapid application of the brakes.

In addition to the air each car is equipped with a hand brake that is set when we tie the train down for the night.

Terms

Railroad workers as well as hobos had their own language. Here are a few terms just for fun but if you are interested in learning more about railroads there are many sites on the internet that cater to enthusiasts.

A-No.1 -"number one man" , later came to mean, "all right (or okay) with me." , thumbs up.

Adam and Eve on a raft - Two fried eggs on toast. "Wreck 'em" if they are scrambled. "With their eyes open," if not.

Alligator bait - Fried or stewed liver. Too costly for hobos.

Axle grease - Butter. Sometimes called plaster.

Brakemen – Baby Lifter .

Caboose – Brain box.

Coffin nail -- cigarettes.

Conductor – ram-rod, skipper, the brains, No sweat.

Cub — New person on the railroad.

Deadhead – RR employee traveling as a passenger.

Engineer – Hogger, Hoghead.

Foamer -- from FOMITE " Fanatically Obnoxious Mentally Incompetent Train Enthusiast". (No disrespect)

Gandy dancer - worker who laid sections of rail. Named from Gandy Mfg Co. that made track tools.

Grade -- The ratio of elevation gained or lost per distance traveled measured in feet, as a percent "%".

Hog – Locomotive.

Jerkwater Town — A small town with few facilities, identified on the railroad by a water plug only.

Old Head – One who has been around long enough to become familiar with his work or who 'has his head cut in' knows how to do his job well. (insult)

Piglet – Engineer Trainee.

Mountain Pay — Overtime.

Highball — Signal to proceed at maximum speed. Station agent would hoist a large ball up a pole so engineer could see and train to pass without stopping.

Ticket Punch

Ticket punching in the United States began in the 1860's. The conductor or someone on his behalf would cancel out the passenger ticket by punching a hole into it. The conductors hole punch was a vital form of identification, each conductor had his  own specifically shaped hole punch that identified them. It was up to the conductor to ensure that every passenger paid proper passage as this revenue was important.

Ticket punching is still used today but on the tourist excursions it is mostly for fun and educational purposes, however it sometimes brings a smile especially since we do NOT throw people from the train.

Pocket Watch

Most recognizable by the chain hanging from the conducts vest pocket is the pocket watch. It is very important that the conductor and engineer keep the same time throughout the run; the crew regularly synchronize their  time pieces to a standard clock. Every crew member is expected to supply their own time piece and is responsible for its accuracy. The railroad in 1883 introduced standardized "Railroad time" and the four time zones we use in the United States today. Before the standard cities kept local time and coordination for long distances was almost impossible. There were several train crashes involving trains keeping different times.

Conductor's Cap

The conductor can be recognized by the "badge of office" traditional black hat with gold trim. A symbol of the passenger train conductor and used throughout North America starting in the 1870's. Other trades such as porter or agent as well as trolley car operators use the same style cap.

Communications

Radios are regularly used in connection with train operations. On a train that consists of ten 80ft. cars the engineer cannot see everything that is happening on the ground at the opposite end or inside the cars so his instructions must be clear and expected. The crew meets before each trip to discuss assignments and plans for the day; the conductor coordinates all these activities. Hand signals as they were used long ago are still an option should radio communications be interrupted. The crew must first meet and agree on a plan that hand signals will then be used. Part of the regular rules training each year includes going over the hand signals in case they're needed.

Crew

The crew today will include an engineer, who is a employee of Georgia Northeastern Railroad and operates the locomotive. There are several safety car hosts who assist with loading, promote safety, and answer questions. The conductor is in charge of the train, responsible for the safety of its passengers, crew, and public relations. There are also two or more Trainmen recognizable by wearing black hats, who assist with train operations and movement. One trainman rides in the engine while the other calls signals to the engineer in route from inside the train. Operating crews have to take annual classroom instruction and pass a safety operating rules test.

Squeal of the wheels

You may notice a squealing sound, as if the engineer is riding the brakes. This squealing sound is noticeable as the train rounds a curve, and as you well know, there are many of those on our trip. The fact is.... This is 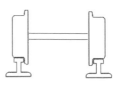 not the brakes at all; instead, it is the flanged wheels of the car rubbing against the inside crown of the rail. Why does this happen? Under each car is a set of "trucks" upon which the car rides. Our cars have two axle trucks, which means that there are two axles affixed together to form a single unit. The length of the truck assemblies, combined with the length of our cars and the sharpness of the curves, means that as the train rounds a curve opposite corners of the flanged wheels of the truck rub against the inside crown of the rail, causing the squealing sound. One might rightfully wonder that if there is that much squealing, there must be quite a bit of wear and friction involved. This is true. If there is wear and friction, then the obvious solution is to oil or grease the rubbing surfaces. This also is true. Yes... the track crew does indeed grease the rails in areas that rubbing and friction occur.

Ron Wallace article

Gauge

The gauge is the distance between the inside edges of the rail. The U.S. as well as three-fifths of the world uses Standard Gauge (4 ft. 8.5 in. or 1.4 meters). This odd number was brought to us from Britain in 1829 when locomotives were imported and the rails had to match.

Vehicles such as chariots, carts or carriages in early transportation were pulled primarily by horses. The speed at which the vehicles could travel, weight a horse could pull, and arrangement that could be handled by a single driver dictated the width of the axle. Later tramways were built with the same jigs and tools that were used to build wagons. So the locomotives built by the British were made with these same measurements. Later American technology enhancements continued to use this common length.

Narrow gauge used in the U.S. in the last decade of the 19th century measured 3 ft 6 in. and in many cases only 2ft. The benefits were shorter-radius turns, cheaper to build and operate. On the down side narrow gauge can only handle lower hauling capacity at slower speeds.

The original line used today was built as narrow gauge and then upgraded much later to standard gauge. Since money was scarce as it was for many railroads across the country at that time, our route took many turns to avoid obstacles because it was cheaper to go around rather than through them. This was one of the key reasons for the original line to be abandoned yet makes it perfect for tourism. Our passenger cars are longer today and have speed restrictions that make it perfect for taking a leisurely trip that gives plenty of time for pictures.

Hobo Signs

A Hobo was an independent and resourceful person who travels for work. The American Hobo "Knights of the road" communicated through a system of marks (Hobo Signs). This code gave information or warnings to others. Written in chalk or coal they let fellow Hobos know what to expect. We have produced only one here for fun at the holding tank dump location depicting bad water.

During the early 1880's times were hard and no one had the money to go places or pay for a ticket to get there. Hoboes took to the rails in great numbers and people in rural communities would help by giving them jobs during harvest time. During the great depression they depicted a way of life many Americans could relate to as thousands of women and children also traveled the rails.

They lived in camps, did not use real names (although some became famous) and followed rules. There was no breaking into homes or threatening people. Offenses could bring heavy punishment by fellow hobo's . Extensive information is available on the internet for those interested.

Mulligan stew (hobo stew) was made from the combined contributions of any Hobo who wanted to eat some. A pot of stew was refreshed by a scrap of meat, a biscuit, or wilted vegetables from a garden. The Hoboes essentials were most importantly water and something to start a fire with but also included a can opener, a knife, a spoon, and candles.

"King of the Road" was a song written by Roger Miller that depicted a lifestyle but the name was also an honor given by unofficial vote of the Hoboes on the road that is the best educated, experienced and most respected of all.

Ticket to Ride

There is no assigned seating in any of the cars. We do however suggest changing sides on the way back so that everyone gets an opportunity to see all of the sights. So come aboard, settle in and meet some new friends.

Tickets are only good for the date printed and you must ride in the car assigned because so many trips sell out. The car number and boarding time also

```
BRSR welcomes          800-934-1898        XV
STRAUB/PASSES

        FRIDAY, 11:00am
            VOLUNTEER

May 07, 2004  OPEN AIR 2975
Boarding 10:40 am              69938-1        69938-1

                                              05/07/04
1-800-934-1898    VISIT DEPOT GIFT SHOP
```

appear on the ticket. Keep it handy as the conductor will come around once we leave the station to punch it out. Be sure to hang on to your stub, it will be a great addition to your scrap book.

Throughout the years many of the local businesses have supported the railroad by giving discounts on meals or merchandise to ticket holders. Ask your car host what businesses are participating in discounts at the time of your ride, show them the stub and save some money. Reservations are not required but it is highly recommended to pre-purchase and pick-up before the trip, that way you are assured of a ticket to ride.

Volunteers

Everyone except the engineer and concession staff are volunteers. Ever since the idea emerged to start a tourist rail excursion volunteers have played a vital part. They shared a love for railroading and a common goal to help re-establish a line in the North Georgia Mountains. In the early years, it was mostly Atlanta Chapter NRHS members but has shifted to more local residents in current years. There are many of the original group that still come back year after year. We also see new faces every year.

They have helped maintain, rework and clean some of the equipment. They have enjoyed special trips, deck parties and luncheons over the years. Everyone keeps coming back because it is fun, relaxing and we are family. If you would like to become part of the family you will be welcomed. Just make it known you are interested to any of the crew and they will put you in touch with the volunteer coordinator.

Each volunteer starts off with some basic training and learns what to expect on a trip as a safety car host. The car host assists passengers on and off the train and provides information during the journey. Each trip starts with a safety briefing to reinforce our training. After you have gotten the routine down and are interested in some additional responsibilities you are welcome to attend a yearly training session and become qualified as trainman. It's not for everyone and many of the volunteers just love the freedom and less time commitment of being a car host. Either way we want people to enjoy working all the positions of the crew. After you have become an accomplished trainman you can choose to qualify as conductor. That's all it takes, a little time and commitment. For your time and commitment you also receive benefits so don't hesitate to ask a volunteer for more information.

I became a volunteer in the year 2000 when my friend Del Kittendorf convinced me it was fun and worthwhile. He said "there is not a better bunch of folks to work with." My family and I volunteered together coming into the mountains enjoying the scenery, local activities, and camaraderie. I took the additional training and worked my way from trainman to conductor over the next few years. Where else can someone with a computer background get to work with vintage locomotives? The folks at GNRR have worked with us year after year to give us the foundation needed to safely run the train. We trade off jobs with experienced conductors so that everyone gets an opportunity to learn and gain their own experience.

One memorable trip for me was a log run south out of Blue Ridge to Tate with five loaded log cars. Calvin Lee, Carl Hyman and I encountered several empty gravel cars along the way that we had to shove several miles before the train could be reconfigured at the rock quarry. After switching cars around by GNRR we were on our way pulling five loaded log cars and three full gravel cars up the hill past Twin Mountain Lake in Talking Rock almost to Tate. The load was too much for two locomotives on this particular day and a third locomotive was brought down to as-sist. We never made it to Tate that hot summer day. Calvin lost his fight with cancer several years later but I will always remember him and that trip as a highlight of my railroad adventures.

Volunteers   89

2008 Group Photo

The Trainman and Conductor group photo has been a tradition over the past few years.

First Row: Ray Leader, Lora Huster, Larry Dyer, Anne Hymen, Carl Hymen, Jeff Knowles, Pat Brady, Jonathan Deitch

Second Row: Alan Czeck, Barry Vincent, Dick Burnett, Don Anderson, David Shuman, Rae Breed, Rae Ann Straub, Rick Straub, John Davis, Joe Brandon

Third Row: Joe King, Ron Graner, Chuck Nutting, Jack Warner, Mike Morrey, Leonard Zeh, Scottie Wershing, Pat Moore, Charles Garland

Back Row: Ron Long, David Ashworth, Charles Ecker Ron Huster, Del Kittendorf, Bob Ciminel, Gragg Robinson, Ron Wallace, Bruce Fielding

Upper Row:
Bob Brackett , Michael Fuchcar, Mike Shaw

Photo by Chris Brackett

The first edition contained the 2007 group photo. It has been retained on **page 94** with the following cast.

First Row: Jonathan Deitch , Anne Hymen , Rae Breed Pat Brady , Lora Huster , Larry Dyer
Second Row: Ron Huster , Bruce Fielding , Ron Wallace Don Anderson , Leonard Zeh , Jack Warner, David Ashworth, Del Kittendorf
Third Row: Ray Leader, Joe Brandon, Chuck Nutting , Pat Moore, Judy King , Ron Graner, Dick Wood, Dick Burnett John Davis , Bob Brackett , Rick Straub
Back Row: Bob Ciminel, Mike Morrey, Jeff Knowles, Joe King Barry Vincent. Photo by Michael Pierce

Volunteer Photo's from various sources

2007 Trainman and Conductor photo. (names on page 91)

Blue Ridge Scenic Railway

Brscenic web page featuring Calvin Lee

GNRR web image by Mike Morrey

The **Georgia Northeastern Railroad, Inc.** (GNRR) operates ~100 miles of trackage from our interchange with CSX Transportation at Marietta, to McCaysville, Georgia. We occupy the old Louisville and Nashville Railroad's "Hook And Eye" line.

We are classified by the Association of American Railroads as a "shortline railroad" This classification is based on annual revenues and car loadings.

We operate the Blue Ridge Scenic Railway presenting riders with a journey along the Toccoa River in the beautiful North Georgia Mountains. The GNRR is locally owned. Its employees are all local folks, and you will find that doing business with us is a real pleasure.

We are always anxious to have potential customers check with our present customers to learn first hand how customized personal service can enhance their business. The GNRR has rail accessible industrial sites available along our trackage.

109 Marr Av. NW
Marietta, Ga 30060
770-428-4784
www.gnrr.com

Thanks for riding with us today.

I hope this guide has added to a pleasurable trip. Until we see you again, have a safe journey and remember, it's always a great day for a train ride.

Ask about other publications made for BRSR

About The Author

Rick Straub joined the volunteer team in 2000. A conductor since 2001, he started the volunteer newsletter in 2005 and helped introduce technology to improve operations. He now lives in the North Georgia Mountains with his wife, Rae Ann and daughter, Carley.

Back cover photo comes from the
Michael Pierce GNRR collection by the artist himself, Michael Pierce.